# CONTENTS

# Introduction

Welcome to the ultimate guide to intermittent fasting for women over 50. In this book, you will find everything you need to know to get started down this amazing path to a better you. Best of all, the information presented herein is done so in a clear and concise manner. All you need is an open mind and the willingness to get started.

This volume is intended for anyone who wants to learn about intermittent fasting, and by extension, how to improve themselves. You will find a trove of information that will help you build on your current self while enabling you to become the best that you can possibly be.

Plus, the information in this book has been the result of years of experience and study. We're not going to be talking about junk science and pop psychology here. We're going to be talking about cold hard facts that will give you the assurance that this dietary approach really works.

So, let's get started on learning all about intermittent fasting. You will soon find that this approach is not only easy to implement but also quite straightforward. You won't need anything fancy to get the most out of intermittent fasting.

The time has come for you to make the most of your own body's power of healing and regeneration, as well as its built-in capabilities to lose weight, shed toxic substances, and trigger processes that have surely been locked up withing you. When you unlock these "hidden" powers, you will feel like a totally new person... regardless of your age.

Do you scratch your head and wonder where to start looking for things to eat during your intermittent fast? Have you spent the day dreading your next fast because you just don't have the energy you need to get through it? Follow this simple, easy-to-follow, 5 ingredients, or less recipes to get the energy you need and the body you desire! You will be glad to notice that there is also a dessert section of this book! That's right, even on a diet you can indulge! This book will give you breakfast, meal, snack, appetizer, and dessert recipes that will make your mouth water and your body melt off pounds!

These recipes include foods that include a composition of relatively low-calories, are high in protein and complex carbs, and offer a nutritious range of ingredients! You will have everything you need to keep your body going and keep it well. All you need is your kitchen, a grocery bag full of ingredients, and the will to make your body strong and healthy!

Want to know the best part? Every recipe in this book is five ingredients or less! They are also all equal to or less than five hundred calories! Your stomach will love the food, but your wallet will love the frugality of the recipes. You can stay healthy while keeping your funds within your budget! Let's take a little sneak peek at what there is in store for you, with over Come on, let's get going!

# Chapter 1: The Basics of Intermittent Fasting

The most common misconception when it comes to intermittent fasting is to stop eating. Sadly, many folks believe that's the core of intermittent fasting. They simply stop eating as they believe this is how they are going to lose weight and obtain the health benefits offered by intermittent fasting.

However, this is not only an irresponsible act, but it's also downright dangerous. You should, by no means, simply stop eating. This will cause your body to panic and eventually enter a state of shock. Depending on your eating habits, this shock could happen within a matter of hours.

You see, the human body evolved over thousands of years on very little food. Nevertheless, over the last two hundred years, or so, food has been relatively abundant around the world. This is a stark contrast to the way our ancestors lived. This has led us to get used to eating three times a day and snacking in between meals. Since the body eventually becomes accustomed to anything, going without food over an extended period of time can cause it to enter a state of shock.

When done right, intermittent fasting unlocks your body's natural ability to repair and detox itself. The secret is to gradually give the body the chance to wean itself from the dependency we have created on food. In particular, the typical western diet is based on sugar, carbs, and high amounts of salt. These substances are highly addictive and cause the body to crave them more and more.

## So, how is intermittent fasting possible then?

It is perfectly possible if you are able to apply a gradual approach. For instance, if you normally eat every couple of hours, you are conditioning your body to crave food on a regular basis. As such, the only time you wouldn't be actively eating is when you are sleeping. That might be anywhere from 4 to 8 hours. That is not enough time to give your body the chance to detox, especially if you have been consuming food throughout the day.

# The Goal of Intermittent Fasting

This is why the goal of intermittent fasting is to reduce caloric intake (by this we mean food and drink) in intervals that can range anywhere from 12 to up to 48 hours. Now, we're not saying that you are going to spend two full days without food. What we are saying is that you should be aiming to go without food as long as you possibly can within reason.

For example, most practitioners of intermittent fasting aim for 12 to 16-hour fasts. This, coupled with good nutrition, allows them to unlock the health benefits that come from intermittent fasting. The best part is that you don't need to fast that long every day to unlock these benefits. What you are essentially doing is giving your metabolism a breather every few days.

When you break it down, a 12-hour fast really isn't that tough. If we assume that you sleep 8 full hours, all you have to do is tack on 4 more hours on top of your 8 hours of sleep. For instance, you could have dinner, wait two hours, go to sleep, and then wait another two hours after rising to have breakfast.

That's a 12-hour fast right there!

Another common misconception is that you are not allowed to consume anything during the time that you are fasting.

That could not be farther from the truth.

In fact, when you are on your fast, you can consume water, tea, or coffee so long as it does not contain anything additional to the beverage itself. You see, water, tea, and coffee don't actually have any calories in them. The calories add up when you combine milk, cream, and sugar. Water, especially, is a great way to get through periods of fasting as it is vital to stay hydrated.

# It's All About Willpower

Additionally, intermittent fasting is all about willpower. It might seem like a stretch for you to go 12 hours without food at this point. But when you break it down to manageable chunks, you'll see that it's all about making to a conscious choice to withhold consuming food for a couple of hours at a time. Of course, it may seem daunting, but it is certainly doable.

The trick here is to gradually work your way up. At first, you may only be able to put in an 8-hour fast. For instance, you have dinner a couple of hours before going to bed, sleep 6 hours, and then have something immediately after waking up.

# That's a fine start.

It could be that you can muster up 10 hours, that is, your 8-hour sleep plus one hour before bedtime and one hour after waking. If you can do that, you are well on your way to mastering intermittent fasting. The best thing about it is that you don't need to do this every day. All you need is to make a conscious effort to actively fast two to three times a week. This is especially true when you are shooting for something like a 16-hour fast.

## Something to Watch Out for

Moreover, it's important to note that you should not fast during your busiest or most demanding days. The reason for this is that energy requirements your body has during busy days may leave you depleted. Hence, this is not a good approach.

Lastly, if you are considering a fast during your waking hours, please make sure that you are in a position in which you can manage any possible side effects. For instance, some folks feel dizzy, tired, or even cranky when they go without food. In particular, if you consume high levels of sugar and carbs, you may experience withdrawal symptoms if you go too long without these foods. So, do take that into consideration. This is why we recommend using your sleeping hours toward your intermittent fasting goal. That way, you will be able to unlock the benefits of the intermittent fasting approach without making it any harder than it has to be.

# Chapter 2: The Science of Intermittent Fasting

Many detractors of the intermittent fasting approach dismiss it as dietary mumbo-jumbo. They claim that it's a fad diet. In other cases, you might hear experts claiming that it's dangerous to go without food for too long.

That last point is actually true. And, we have discussed the reasons for it.

When you break down the science that supports intermittent fasting, you find that fasting, that is going without food, is rooted in our genetic makeup. Humans evolved on needing very little food. This is why the body hoards calories as much as it can.

So, let's go back to our cave-dweller days to put that last point into perspective.

In those days, humans didn't eat every day, much less three times a day. Early humans had to do with whatever food they could find. That often meant going days without caloric consumption. That meant that the body had to become very efficient at using as little calories as it could to power the entire body while saving as much as it could. After all, the body had no way of determining when it would eat again.

This evolutionary trait led the body to develop store calories by way of fat. Fat is a substance which is built from glucose. Glucose is the chemical the metabolism creates from the food that is consumed. Ultimately, all unused glucose is stored as fat. This is why folks tend to gain so much weight when they consume large amounts of sugar and carbs.

How so?

Sugar and carbs are very easy for the body to process and convert into glucose. The downside is that they require insulin to be processed. This doesn't occur with fat and protein. Fat, such as olive oil, is used by the body to produce a number of other chemicals. In excess, it is converted into reserve calories. Protein (such as meat) is used up to power muscles. Protein cannot be stored. So, any excess protein is excreted by the body, usually through the urine.

## Intermittent Fasting and Weight Loss

Weight loss occurs when the body needs to use up its reserves to fuel the body. This only happens when there is no other caloric intake. In a manner of speaking, it's like having a production line that sends goods to a warehouse. The warehouse will remain relatively empty if the production line produces just enough to keep up with demand. If the production line produces too many goods, then the warehouse will eventually get full. Now, imagine if the warehouse had the ability to bulge to any size needed to accommodate the ever-increasing production.

## This is what happens when you consume too many calories.

Therefore, the solution is to create a caloric deficit. This can be done by temporarily shutting down the production line. If the production line is shut down, the only choice the warehouse is to using existing stock items to meet customer demands.

This analogy highlights what the body must do with its fat stores in order to keep the body running in the absence of incoming food. The caloric deficit created by the lack of intake allows stored up calories to be used.

## Intermittent Fasting and Detoxing

One of the greatest benefits that come from intermittent fasting is detoxing. The rationale behind this is that when the metabolism does not need process food, it can then switch to "cleaning up" the system. This is an important function that often gets overlooked. We tend to think that what we eat gets used up and what doesn't will eventually come out.

## However, it doesn't always come out...

In fact, digested and undigested food can remain in the digestive tract for several days. Needless to say, this is not a good thing. So, when the digestive system is not actively digesting food, this enables it to process whatever is leftover in the system. This is why drinking plenty of water during fasting periods can cause you to go to the bathroom quite often.

The great benefit is that when your digestive system is cleaned up, it allows your metabolism to more actively process new food that comes in. This is why it leads to increased levels of energy while enabling the body to make better use of the nutrients in the food you consume.

## Increased Energy

Another great effect stemming from intermittent fasting is increased energy. As your metabolism becomes more efficient at processing the reduced amount of food intake, it is able to extract the maximum amount of calories it can. But since you aren't accumulating excess calories, the body needs to use them use up in order to keep the whole system rolling. This is why folks who go on the intermittent fasting approach indicate they feel more active, especially after meals, rather than drowsy and lazy.

What you are seeing is your metabolism squeezing as much as it can out of the food you consume. So, a faster metabolism is a direct consequence of intermittent fasting. Additionally, if the food you eat doesn't provide enough calories, then your body can just dip into its reserves. Either way, your metabolism has no choice but to become more efficient at managing its energy production.

## Better Nutrition

When your body undergoes a detox, it allows your intestines to flush out any residue. This is important as the intestinal tract is where nutrition is absorbed. So, if the plumbing is backed up, so to speak, then it is very hard for the body to absorb nutrients properly. Thus, cleaning up the pipes is essential to facilitating this process.

The great thing about intermittent fasting is that you don't need to go on a juice cleanse or take any additional medication. The body knows exactly what to do. All you need is to drink plenty of water in order to ensure that you stay hydrated. Beyond that, your body will progressively improve its ability to absorb nutrition, thereby improving your overall health and wellness.

# Chapter 3: Types of Intermittent Fasting Approaches for Women

If you thought that intermittent fasting was a one-size-fits-all approach, you might be surprised to find that there are different ways of going about it. While the underlying science and rationale behind it points to the same principles, there are various ways in which you can unlock the benefits that come with intermittent fasting.

Now, it should be noted that you should give each one of these approaches a try but avoid mixing them up. If you try to "mix and match" the guidelines for each of these methods, then you might not get the results you seek. So, it's best to try one out and the transition into another.

Let's take a look then at four effective ways in which you can practice intermittent fasting.

## Twice a Week (The 5:2 Method)

This method gets its name from the "five days eat, two days fast" approach. This means that out of a regular sever-day week, you'll eat normally for five days while fasting for two. The main trick here is to choose two days during which you can consistently fast. Ideally, you would be able to build a discipline that would enable you to train your body to recognize the days on which you will be fasting.

Also, you should at least have one non-fasting day in between both of your fast days. This is done to avoid going a total of 48 hours with very little to no caloric intake. During your fasting days, you are generally permitted a single meal of roughly 200 to 300 calories max. For instance, a bowl of fruit and yogurt would be enough to meet this requirement. For the rest of the day, you would consume plenty of water, tea, or coffee. However, it's best to avoid too much coffee as it has a diuretic effect.

Also, it's a good idea to ramp down on your meals on the day before you fast and then gradually ramp up on the day you break the fast. If you choose to have a full meal right after coming out of a fast, you might get sick.

## Alternating Days

This method is definitely not for beginners. In this method, you are essentially alternating your fast days. For example, Monday would be a regular day, then Tuesday a fast day, Wednesday regular, Thursday fast, Saturday regular, Sunday fast, and so on.

In this method, you limit your caloric intake to an absolute maximum of 500 calories on a fast day. Then, you resume a regular diet (hopefully very healthy) on non-fast days. It should be noted that this approach may interfere with your plans, particularly if you like to go out for a meal on the weekend. Nevertheless, you can certainly plan your lifestyle around it so that you can gain the maximum amount of benefits.

The important thing with the alternating days intermittent fasting method is consistency. At first, you may not be able to stick to the 500 calories, but you might be able to gradually reduce your portion size, then cut down to two meals and then cut down to a single meal or two very light snacks.

## Time Restricted Method

In this method, as its name suggests, you are restricting all caloric intake for a specific amount of time. Unlike the previous two methods, you are not permitted to consume anything aside from liquids during this time.

An example of this is the 16/8 method. In the 16/8 method, you fast for 16 hours and eat for 8. Now, the idea is not to binge during your eating window. Rather, you want to keep things as light as possible. That way, you can give your metabolism a chance to ramp down. Other combinations include 14/10 (14 hours fast, 10 eat) 18/6, and 20/4. It is not recommended to fast for 24 hours in a row as this could potentially be dangerous for you.

Also, this method is generally practiced once or twice a week. There is no need to fast on the exact same days all the time, though it is helpful to build consistency. Additionally, this approach is not generally practiced more than twice a week. If you choose to go for three days a week, please ensure that you are comfortable with this frequency. Anything beyond three days a week is simply dangerous and should not be attempted.

## Eat-Stop-Eat or The 24-Hour Fast

This method is the most extreme method you can find. It should only be done by truly experienced practitioners of the intermittent fasting approach. Plus, you need to build your stamina up to get to this level. For instance, some individuals start off with a 12/12 approach, then 14/10, 16/8, 18/6, 20/4, and then hit the 24-hour mark.

Earlier, we mentioned that going without food for 24 hours can be dangerous. As such, you may experience symptoms like dizziness, fatigue, headaches, and if you are hooked on sugar and carbs, you may experience withdrawal symptoms (irritability, anxiety, and even severe headaches).

On the whole, this approach is not recommended unless it is done under medical supervision. This is especially true if you have any kind of medical condition. In such cases, it might be wise to forego attempting this method. Nevertheless, you might want to give it a try as a means of a challenge. While there are individuals who practice this approach on a regular basis, say twice a week, most practitioners engage in it roughly once or twice a month.

Furthermore, please make sure to ramp down your caloric intake on the day before your fast and gradually ramp up your caloric intake during the day after. Plus, make sure to keep your physical activity moderate. This type of challenge is best done at home and in the company of others who can keep an eye on you. If you attempt this challenge, be ready to have a very light meal, should you feel any of the symptoms described earlier. For instance, fruit and yogurt is a great way to help you regain stability.

# Chapter 4: Food to Eat and Avoid in Intermittent Fasting

The main goal of intermittent fasting is to embrace a healthier lifestyle. This means that it should be part of a holistic approach that leads to an overall healthier lifestyle. As such, it's important for you to really take a deep look at what you are eating on non-fast days. In addition, regular exercise and cutting back on harmful substances like cigarettes and alcohol will go a long way toward promoting a host of health benefits.

This is why it's important for you to focus on foods which you should eat and which ones you should. After all, you would only be hurting yourself if you binge on non-fast days and then suddenly flip off the switch on fast days. The gains which you could make in a few weeks of intermittent fasting can be derailed by a couple of binge sessions.

So, let's take a look at foods which you should embrace and the ones which you shouldn't. Ideally, this will become part of your healthier lifestyle plan.

## Foods to Embrace

Ideally, intermittent fasting will become part of an overall healthy lifestyle for you. This means that you would be cutting out certain foods that are rather harmful (in excess, of course) and embracing foods that are healthy.

Now, it should be said that during non-fasting days, there are no restrictions on what you can eat. That's why the ideal way to go is to reduce your consumption of foods high in carbs and sugar while embracing fresh foods and lean meats. So, let's take a look at the foods which you ought to make mainstays of your regular diet:

- Fresh fruits. The best kind would be fresh without any additives or extra sugar.
- Raw vegetables. Nothing frozen. The fresher the better, and they conserve their nutrients much better. Additionally, these can be cooked and consumed on a regular basis.
- Lean meat. There are no restrictions on the type of meat you can eat. However, meat that's too fatty may elevate your cholesterol to unhealthy levels.
- Whole grains. This is the best way to consume your favorite foods. Whole grains are loaded with fiber while also reducing the amount of carbs you consume. Carbs from vegetables and whole grains are far more digestible by the body and lead to less accumulation of fat in the body.
- Nuts. Nuts are a good source of healthy fats and protein. They are great during ramp up and ramp down times. So, definitely incorporate them into your diet.

As we have mentioned before, the intermittent fasting approach does not openly restrict any foods. So, it's a question of limiting the amount of white, starchy foods and sugar while increasing the amount of fresh foods, lean meats, whole grains, and nuts that you consume. When you do this, you give your body the chance to work with quality materials during its repair process.

# Foods to Avoid

You often hear health experts demonizing sugar and carbs. Now, it should be said that sugar and carbs are not necessarily bad. They become a problem when they are consumed in excess. When you eat too many of these foods, your body has to play catchup. Naturally, this is where you accumulate fat, gain weight, and see the negative effects of an unhealthy diet.

## So, the intermittent fasting approach calls for you to avoid, or at least significantly reduce, the following foods:

- •White starchy foods. This includes past and potatoes. Starch is metabolized as glucose and immediately goes into fat stores.
- Foods loaded with carbs. White bread, or anything baked, is usually loaded with a high amount of carbs.
- Greasy foods. Deep-fried and very greasy foods, while tasty, are high in unhealthy fats. These types of fats lead to high cholesterol. These foods are enemy number one for blood vessel health. They generally lead to poor circulation.
- Salty foods. There's nothing wrong with salt unless you eat too much of it. Salting foods to taste is fine. However, excessively salty foods are not only addictive, but they affect your blood pressure and heart health. It's best to switch to sea salt as it contains less sodium.
- Sugary drinks and alcohol. By "sugary," we mean things like sodas and iced teas. These are loaded with sugar and other chemicals. Also, alcoholic beverages end up accumulating fat in a heartbeat. Now, consuming moderate amounts of alcohol is perfectly fine (1 to 2 drinks per week). In fact, a glass of wine will do a great number on your heart. However, it's excessive alcohol consumption that leads to increased fat gains. The reasoning behind this is that alcohol is metabolized by the body the same way sugar is. So, this implies you'll be packing on extra glucose in your system. Also, check with your doctor to see if you have any unknown food allergies. Unfortunately, many folks out there go through their entire lives not knowing they are, in fact, allergic to certain foods. For instance, there are folks who are lactose intolerant but don't know it. Other common food allergies are gluten and corn. In particular, corn allergies can lead to quite a bit of digestive distress and inflammation. This is important to note as many of the foods we consume have corn in them.

Lastly, maintaining a healthy diet is all about exercising moderation and common sense. If you are aware of what foods you should cut down on, then it's best to do so. Now, there's nothing wrong with enjoying your favorite foods. As a matter of fact, intermittent fasting will provide you with the opportunity to push the reset button, so to speak. This means that you would be able to enjoy your favorites without too much guilt. However, if you overdo it, then you will find that you can easily derail the hard work you have put in.

So, please keep in mind that maintaining a balanced diet, as much as possible, in tandem with regular exercise, will make intermittent fasting work very well, thereby producing the results you seek.

# Chapter 5: Most Common Mistakes during Intermittent Fasting

Intermittent fasting is as much science as it is art. Thus, it's important to keep in mind that while there is no "perfect" way of doing it, there are "right" and "wrong" things that you need to watch out for. In this chapter, we are going to focus on the most common mistake that novice practitioners of intermittent fasting make, especially in the early going. Moreover, we're going to be looking at how you can avoid these mistakes.

## Going All in

Perhaps the most common mistake is going "all in" right away. By this, we mean that you set out to do a 10-hour fast, for instance, at the drop of a hat. This is not only counterproductive but also downright dangerous.

You see, when you make the decision to take up intermittent fasting, you need to ease your way into it. You can't just expect to go without food straight away. If you do this, you could put your health at serious risk. The most common symptoms include irritability, dizziness, and even anxiety.

So, the solution to this situation is to ease into intermittent fasting. The best way is to gradually spread yourself out so that you can confidently start out with an 8-hour fast. If you are sleeping a full 8 hours on a regular basis, all you need to do is make sure that you don't consume any food at least an hour before bedtime. Then, try your best to avoid consuming any food until at least 30 minutes after rising.

Please make sure to pace yourself in order to avoid the most unpleasant symptoms that come when you go too long without food.

## Binging Before and After Fasting

A common mistake is having a big meal right before a fast. The logic here is that you are "stocking up" for the time you won't be eating. That is not only a mistake, but it's also counterproductive. When you do this, your body goes out of whack. It might think that there is something wrong and may choose to hoard calories instead of burning them off.

By the same token, binging after a fasting day is a one-way ticket to digestive distress. It's always a good idea to have a very light meal right after a fast. That way, you can give your metabolism and digestive system a chance to adjust to food again. The longer you go without food, the easier you need to take it on your digestive system.

## Fasting Too Often

Those intermittent fasting practitioners that believe that "more is better" are only asking for trouble. When you fast too often, your body may enter starvation mode. This means that the body thinks that something is going on, and food is scarce. So rather than use up fat stores, the body begins to hoard as much as it can. This is where intermittent fasting practitioners plateau and subsequently begin gaining weight.

This is why the recommended guideline is to fast two times a week, three times tops. Ideally, you would leave at least a couple of days in between fasts. If you are able to accustom your body to consume less food, then your body won't think that there is something wrong when you fast. It will simply draw on its stores. In this manner, you can avoid triggering starvation mode.

## Not Fasting Enough

While this isn't a mistake per se, it is simply not the most efficient practice. Not fasting enough means fasting once or twice a month. Please note that 24-hour fasts, the ones which are recommended once a month, are fasts which are done in addition to regular fast days. Consequently, it's best to have a regular routine. This will allow your body to find a rhythm that will ensure that you get the most out of your intermittent fasting practice.

Additionally, please try to avoid an irregular routine. For instance, you decide to fast for three days a week over a four-week period, and then go weeks without fasting. What this will do is throw your body out of whack. When the body is out of whack, it will naturally resort to starvation mode. Moreover, you may end up experiencing some of the most unpleasant symptoms that come when you don't eat. So, this is why we advocate having a regular routine as much as possible.

## Falling Into a Predictable Routine

While routines are important, the body may also fall into a predictable rut if you maintain the same routine for too long. When the body eventually gets used to the new routine, you may find that you plateau in your weight loss goals. To avoid this, it's important to shake things up a bit.

The most effective way that intermittent fasting practitioners shake off falling into a routine is by switching up their approach. For instance, some folks like to start off with the 5:2 methods. Then, after a three or four-month period, switch to an alternating day fast. After another three or four month, they switch over to the time-restricted method. Once they achieve a high level of proficiency, they may choose to throw in a 24-hour fast every so often.

The rationale behind this is that once the body finally adjusts to the new intermittent fasting approach, things get switched up. In this manner, the metabolism is "on its toes." Of course, the secret to making a smooth transition is to gradually switch from one method to another. This can be done over a two-week period. During that time, you need to ensure that you don't lose track of your progress by binging or cheating on your dietary approach. An example of this is skipping a couple of weeks to give your body a "break" from intermittent fasting. If anything, you will find that after you get used to fasting, you won't need to take a break. Furthermore, on the days in which you enjoy your favorite treats (yes, you can have a couple of drinks or a slice of your favorite cake), you won't feel the least bit guilty. You will already have achieved your fair share of success beforehand.

# Chapter 6: Exercise and Intermittent Fasting

A common concern of novice intermittent fasting practitioners is exercise. There is a myth surrounding exercise in which some so-called experts recommend that folks don't exercise during intermittent fasting days. Some "gurus" even go as far as saying that intermittent fasting practitioners need to "take it easy" otherwise they may experience unpleasant symptoms.

The fact of the matter is that there are no serious restrictions when it comes to exercise and the intermittent fasting approach. However, there are a few precautions that need to be taken in order to ensure that everything goes smoothly.

## Avoid Over-Exerting Yourself on Fasting Days

Yes, you can exercise on fasting days. However, you need to be careful about not overdoing it. If you practice some kind of strenuous workout routine, then save it for non-fasting days. During fasting days, you might want to go about something a little lighter. Common exercise routines for fasting days include yoga, Pilates, or light aerobic exercise such as walking.

Starting out, the 5:2 methods works very well with exercise. Since this method enables you to consume food on fasting days, you can schedule light meals around your workout. Additionally, you must stay hydrated in order to avoid any unpleasant effects such as dehydration, dizziness, lightheadedness, or just plain fatigue.

Weight training is also possible on fasting days; just don't push it too much. Folks who exercise on fasting days use this day to ramp down after tough workouts or as a means of giving their muscles a break, but still keeping active.

## Don't Drink Too Much Water

A very common mistake that folks make is drinking too much water during a workout on a fasting day. Yes, water is important. However, drinking too of it may cause you to lose minerals and electrolytes. This can lead to dizziness and fatigue. So, the issue here leads folks to blame intermittent fasting for their feelings when, in reality, it's just the effect of drinking too much water.

A good solution on fasting days is to drink lemon water instead of regular water. A great lemon or lime water mix includes squeezing one lemon, or a couple of regular limes, into about a half-liter of water. If you like, you can drink unsweetened. If you want to sweeten it up just a bit, add a spoonful of honey. Also, don't forget to add a pinch of salt. This mixture will help you balance out your minerals and electrolytes, particularly during a good workout.

Please avoid consuming sports drinks as they contain too much unnecessary sugar. Additionally, some folks like to consume rehydration salts during fast days. This is done to avoid any possibility of mineral loss. Ultimately, the best thing to do is to avoid energy or rehydration drinks if possible.

# Don't Exercise During a 24-Hour Fast

This would be the only time when we wouldn't recommend you to exercise. During a 24-hour fast, your body is a state of complete standby. Even if you spread 500 calories throughout the 24-hour period, it would still make it hard for you to avoid any unpleasant symptoms. Mainly, the big issue here is feeling fatigued early on.

## Think about this situation:

You enter the 24-hour fast and choose to have a regular gym workout. Even if you are in fabulous shape, the chances are that your energy may not last you through the entire workout. In the end, you might end up feeling starved and in need of some quick food energy. So, you might end up consuming the first thing you run into, thereby breaking the fast.

On the flip side, let's assume you choose to take it easy. Depending on your physical condition, that might leave you feeling hungry and thirsty. In these situations, you would need to keep a healthy snack on hand to help you curb your appetite. However, that may not be enough to get you through the entire 24-hour window. The end result may be breaking the fast.

On the whole, it is not recommended to exercise during a 24-hour fast. If anything, it might be a good idea to use this day as a rest and recovery day. In those cases, the 24-hour fast can work wonders. Not only will you be able to get through the entire period, but you will also feel refreshed and energized. So, it's always best to avoid exercise during a 24-hour fast.

# The Main Takeaway

Exercising on fasting days is perfectly fine. However, you need to be aware of the fact that you can't overdo it. Unless you are used to strenuous exercise on little food, it might be best to ramp up physical activity during a fast. In fact, most individuals like to set up their fasting days on days in which they don't plan to have a lot of physical activity. In fact, some folks avoid fasting on days when they know they have a busy schedule at work.

Overall, there are no serious restrictions. But the main thing to keep in mind is avoiding dehydration. If you are not careful with keeping yourself properly hydrated, you may end up having some serious symptoms. Then, you may attribute them to the diet, when in reality, it was just the result of not managing your hydration right.

Then again, some intermittent fasting practitioners like to gradually build up the intensity of their workouts on fasting days. That way, they can give their body the opportunity to slowly become adjusted to higher physical demands on lower caloric intake. As always, it's best to check with your doctor before attempting to ramp up your physical activity during fast days. While you should not experience any negative symptoms, it's always best to err on the side of caution. As long as you play it safe, you should have no concerns about enjoying the benefits of intermittent fasting and regular exercise.

# Chapter 7: Insider Secrets of Intermittent Fasting

When setting out on your intermittent fasting journey, it's important to keep in mind that success is built on a number of good practices. That's why this chapter is about providing you with insider secrets that will set you up for success no matter where you are coming from.

The best part is that these secrets are really easy to implement into your routine. So, don't be afraid to give them a try.

The Difference Between Needing and Wanting to Eat

It is of the utmost importance for you to recognize when you are really hungry and when you think you are hungry.

## There is a huge difference here.

Often, we fall into the trap of eating without actually being hungry. If you are guilty of this, it's time that you started noticing what triggers these cravings. For instance, if you overeat when you are anxious, then it might be a good idea for you to pay close attention to these instances. That can make a significant difference in your overall success.

## Eat Only When Needed

When you are able to recognize when you eat without begin hungry, you begin to create a discipline in which you eat only when needed. The easiest way to do this is to build a schedule and then stick to it. Building a rather strict schedule will help you accustom your body to eating only when really needed. This approach will go along way in helping your stretch your fasting periods.

## Hydration Is Essential

Throughout this book, we've talked about how essential it is to hydrate during fast days. It is vital for you to make sure that you drink plenty of water. While plain water is perfectly healthy, it should also be mentioned that fruit and vegetable juices are a great source of nutrition.

Ideally, you would consume these juices without any added sugar. Generally speaking, most fruits and vegetables have very little calories. So, you won't blow your calorie budget during fast days. Moreover, most fruits don't have a high glucose content. For instance, apples and lemons don't have much glucose. However, oranges and bananas do. Thus, you want to stick to apple juice and lemon water while cutting down a bit on orange juice. If you can get fresh oranges and squeeze them, you could build a winning formula without consuming needless sugar.

# Take Things Slowly

We've discussed how ramping down prior to a fast and then ramping up following a fast is the best way to go. To make this easier, you could use the following rule of thumb. If you are planning to fast on a Monday, you could ramp down your meals, starting with Sunday's lunch. For example, a wholesome lunch (not overdoing it) followed by a very light dinner roughly two hours before bedtime will help you set yourself up for success. Then, consume plenty of water upon getting up on Monday morning. This will keep you full throughout the early morning. Next, make a plan to consume some fruit or non-fat, unsweetened yogurt. This should give you the caloric intake you need. Assuming you are doing a 12-hour fast, plan to have a very light lunch. That way, you won't be burdening your digestive system following the fast. Lastly, you can have a normal dinner, but without overdoing it. The next day, you can go about your usual eating habits.

With this approach, you will never go wrong. You will always feel comfortable at all times during your fasting days.

# Cut Down on Carbs and Sugar Even on Non-Fast Days

During non-fast days, you are free to have your usual eating regimen. However, it's best to cut down on sugar and carbs since being hooked on these will make it very difficult for you to get through a fasting period. In fact, folks who try to fast while seriously hooked on sugar and carbs often feel anxious and edgy. They even suffer from mild to serious withdrawal symptoms.

So, the best way to go about it is to cut down on your sugar intake well before attempting to go on a full fast. For instance, you can cut down on your portion sizes roughly two weeks before attempting to do your first fast. That way, you can begin the detoxing process while avoiding any nasty withdrawal symptoms.

# Keep Track of Your Achievements

We're going old school here. Keep track of your achievements by using a regular notebook. There is something about writing things down on paper that makes it highly personal. When you do this, you are able to see how you have been progressing. Make sure to write down the date and the length of each fast. Also, include some notes about the things that went right and the things that didn't go right. That way, you can see how your intermittent fasting regimen has been affecting you both positively and negatively.

Over time, you can look back to see the progress you have made. This is why journaling can be one of the most significant things that you can do to give yourself the boost you need, especially when you are feeling down. We don't recommend using note-taking or journaling apps on your phone or tablet as they tend to be rather impersonal. Additionally, a notebook or diary is a very personal item. Please bear in mind that this is a very personal journey. As a result, chronicling your achievements will enable you to keep things closer to heart.

## Easy & Quick Healthy Weight Lose Recipes.........................

# Chapter 1

## Breakfast

The most important meal of the day is even more important for intermittent fasters. Breakfast is specifically timed with fasting, and it is the point in time where you break your previously-determined time period of fasting. What you put in your body during this time is critical to kickstarting your metabolism and setting you up for a great day.

## Bulletproof Coffee

How many people it serves: 1
Time to prepare and cook this recipe: 7 minutes
Calorie content: approx. 214

### Ingredients:

- 1.0 tbsp MTC oil
- 1.0 tbsp butter, unsalted (grass-fed is best, and is very smooth)
- 1.0 mug consisting of 12 oz of your favorite coffee

### Instructions:

1. Brew yourself a fine cup of coffee.
2. Mix that butter in until it melts just right!
3. Add your tablespoon of MTC oil, and voila! You have bulletproof coffee.

# Peanut Butter Banana
# Oatmeal With Chia

How many people it serves: 2
Time to prepare and cook this recipe: 10 minutes
Calorie content: approx. 370

## Ingredients:

- 2.0 tbsp of peanut or similar butter
- 3.0 cups of your favorite non-dairy milk such as almond milk
- 1.0 tbsp of chia seeds
- 1.0 banana cubed or sliced according to preference
- 1.0 cup old fashioned oats

## Instructions:

1. Dump all of your ingredients besides the milk and peanut butter to a sizeable cooking pot.
2. Add the milk gradually to the mixture to ensure even distribution.
3. Stir it all up!
4. Heat the oatmeal mixture over a moderately high temperature for ten minutes.
5. Take the pot off the heated burner and stir the peanut butter into the mixture.
6. Spoon the oatmeal into your favorite bowl and, if desired, scatter a few more chia seeds and splash a bit more almond milk over the top.

# Peanut Butter and Spinach Breakfast Smoothie

How many people it serves: 1
Time to prepare and cook this recipe: 5 minutes
Calorie content: approx. 320

## Ingredients:

- 2.0 cups of spinach
- .75 cups of cold milk of choice, preferably almond milk
- 1.0 hefty tbsp of protein powder, preferably vanilla
- 1.5 tbsp peanut butter, or related nut butter
- 1.5 frozen bananas

## Instructions:

1. Toss everything into your blender and enjoy!

# Chia Seed Pudding
# With Berries

How many people it serves: 1
Time to prepare and cook this recipe: 10 minutes
Calorie content: approx. 240

## Ingredients:

* 1.0 handful of fresh berries of your choice
* .5 tbsp of natural honey
* 8.0 oz of almond milk
* 4.0 tbsp of chia seeds

## Instructions:

1. Stir it all together, except the berries, into a mason jar until all the clumps are gone.
2. Dump the berries on top of the chia pudding.
3. That's it!

# Peach and Blackberry
# Greek Yogurt

How many people it serves: 1
Time to prepare and cook this recipe: 5 minutes
Calorie content: approx. 280

## Ingredients:

* 1.0 tsp of natural honey
* .25 cup of granola
* 1.0 sliced up peach
* .25 cup of fresh, washed blackberries
* 8.0 oz Greek yogurt, plain

## Instructions:

1. Pour the Greek yogurt into your favorite breakfast bowl.
2. Top it off with the blackberries and peach slices.
3. Sprinkle in some granola.
4. Drizzle that honey on top for a sweet final touch!

# Banana Strawberry
# Breakfast Smoothie

How many people it serves: 1
Time to prepare and cook this recipe: 5 minutes
Calorie content: approx. 165

## Ingredients:

- 1.0 tsp natural honey
- 3.0 frozen strawberries
- .33 cup almond milk or milk of choice
- .25 cup Greek yogurt, plain
- 1.0 frozen banana without the peel

## Instructions:

1. Toss it all into your favorite blender and combine it all up! That is all there is to it!

# Breakfast Baked Potato

How many people it serves: 1
Time to prepare and cook this recipe: 20 minutes
Calorie content: approx. 300

## Ingredients:

- 1.0 tbsp cheddar cheese shreds
- 1.0 whole small potato
- 1.0 tsp butter, melted
- 1.0 egg, beaten

## Instructions:

1. Bake your potato.
2. Whisk your egg with seasonings of your choice and scramble it up in a pan at a medium temperature.
3. Slice a slit into your baked potato and pour in the butter until it gets nice and saturated.
4. Fill the potato with the eggs and cover it with the cheddar cheese.
5. Let the cheese melt, then chow down!

# Avocado and Bacon Breakfast Taco

How many people it serves: 1
Time to prepare and cook this recipe: 15 minutes
Calorie content: 300

## Ingredients:

- .5 an avocado, diced up
- 1.0 sliver of bacon
- 2.0 tbsp cheese shreds of choice
- 1.0 flour tortilla

## Instructions:

1. Prep your avocado.
2. Cook your bacon until it sizzles in a pan.
3. Separate the bacon into tiny pieces.
4. Scatter the avocado and bacon onto the tortilla and sprinkle on some cheese.
5. Roll it up and munch away!

# Popsicles, Breakfast-Style

How many people it serves: 6
Time to prepare and cook this recipe: Overnight
Calorie content: approx. 100

## Ingredients:

- 1.5 cups of your favorite fruit or berries
- 1.0 tsp of vanilla
- 2.0 tsp maple syrup, pure
- 1.25 cups of yogurt, plain

## Instructions:

1. Stir everything up in a nice-sized bowl.
2. Pour the mixture into six separate molds for popsicles.
3. Toss the popsicle molds in the freezer and let it set overnight.
4. Pop them out, and enjoy!

# Skinny English Muffins

How many people it serves: 4
Time to prepare and cook this recipe: 45 minutes
Calorie content: approx. 165

## Ingredients:

- 5.0 cups of cauliflower
- 8.0 oz of cheese, cheddar
- 1.0 egg, beaten gently
- .13 tsp of salt

## Instructions:

1. Heat the oven up and ensure that it reaches exactly 425 degrees Fahrenheit.
2. Cover a big baking sheet with parchment paper.
3. Chop up the cauliflower in a food processor until it's nice and rice-like.
4. Heat the cauliflower in a microwave until it's nice and warm.
5. Pat-dry the cauliflower inside some paper towels and make sure as much water as possible is taken out.
6. Toss the cauliflower back into the bowl you microwaved it in, then add the rest of the ingredients and stir them around.
7. Form the dough into nice biscuit shapes and put them on the parchment paper-covered baking sheet.
8. Bake the muffins until they get nice and brown, which should take no more than twenty-five minutes.
9. Let them cool, then enjoy!

# Fruity Cheesecake Delight Toast

How many people it serves: 1
Time to prepare and cook this recipe: 5 minutes
Calorie content: approx. 185

## Ingredients:

- 1.0 sliced up strawberry
- .5 kiwi, sliced up and peeled
- 1.0 piece of wheat bread
- 1.0 tbsp cream cheese
- 2.0 tbsp strawberry Greek yogurt, low-fat

## Instructions:

1. Mix up the yogurt and cheese in a little bowl.
2. Pop the piece of bread in the toaster.
3. Take a butter knife and disperse the mixture evenly on top of the toasted bread.
4. Sprinkle the fruit on top of the toast, and you are ready to eat!

# Banana-Nut Bagel

How many people it serves: 2
Time to prepare and cook this recipe: 5 minutes
Calorie content: approx. 285

## Ingredients:

- 1.0 sliced up banana
- 1.0 divided bagel, toasted
- 1.0 tsp natural honey
- 2.0 tbsp natural peanut butter, or nut butter of choice

## Instructions:

1. Combine up the honey and nut butter in a little bowl.
2. Spread the concoction onto the divided bagel.
3. Add the bananas on the top and enjoy!

# Berries and Cream With a Touch of Lemon

How many people it serves: 4
Time to prepare and cook this recipe: 10 minutes
Calorie content: approx. 175

## Ingredients:

- 16.0 oz blueberries, washed
- 2.0 tsp lemon zest
- 4.0 oz cream cheese
- 1.0 tsp natural honey
- .75 cup of yogurt, vanilla

## Instructions:

1. Excluding the blueberries, blend all of the remaining ingredients up into a nice, light cream.
2. Scoop the lemony cream onto the blueberries and enjoy!

# Nacho Breakfast Toast

How many people it serves: 1
Time to prepare and cook this recipe: 10 minutes
Calorie content: approx. 125

## Ingredients:

- 1.0 tbsp salsa
- 1.0 tbsp cheese of your choice, but Mexican is recommended
- 1.0 piece of toasted wheat bread
- 2.0 tbsp refried beans

## Instructions:

1. Layer the beans and salsa onto your bread.
2. Sprinkle on some cheese.
3. Heat it up in the microwave only long enough to melt the cheese.
4. Slice the bread in half, pick it up, and have your breakfast!

# Avocado Egg Boat

How many people it serves: 2
Time to prepare and cook this recipe: 20 minutes
Calorie content: approx. 200

## Ingredients:

- .12 tsp of salt
- 2.0 eggs
- 1.0 avocado, cut into two halves
- 1.0 tsp of olive oil

## Instructions:

1. Once the pit of the avocado is removed from the halves, separate the two parts of the avocado.
2. Crack each egg into the respective halves of the avocado, making sure to get the egg, including the yolk, into the circular dent left behind by the pit.
3. Sprinkle the salt on top of the egg.
4. Take out a pan and warm the olive oil in it until it starts to heat to a high temperature.
5. Cook the avocado halves in the pan with the egg-filled side down against the heat.
6. Cover the pan with its lid and let the avocados sit in the heat for about five minutes while you turn the temperature down to a low medium.
7. Take the lid off and slide the avocados onto two plates, and enjoy your breakfast!

# Chapter 2

# Meals

These meals are specially designed with complex carbs, protein, and nutrients in mind to keep your body full and running like a well-oiled machine so you can power through your fasts!

## Cajun Salmon With Pineapple Salsa

How many people it serves: 4
Time to prepare and cook this recipe: 20 minutes
Calorie content: approx. 485 (including the rice)

### Ingredients:

- 16.0 oz of your choice of rice, on which to serve the salmon
- Plentiful amounts of pineapple salsa to serve atop the salmon
- 3.0 tbsp Cajun seasoning
- 1.0 tbsp butter or olive oil
- 4.0 salmon filets equaling 6.0 oz each

### Instructions:

1. Massage the Cajun seasoning into the filet of salmon.
2. Take a nice sized, nonstick skillet and melt butter or heat olive oil in it over a temperature of medium intensity.
3. Place the filets of salmon into the skillet and sizzle until they are darkened on the side without the skin.
4. Liberally spread the pineapple salsa over the top surface of the salmon and serve on top of a bed of rice.

# Pesto Spaghetti
# Squash Salad

How many people it serves: 4
Time to prepare and cook this recipe: 45 minutes
Calorie content: approx. 350

## Ingredients:

- 8.0 oz of chopped up sun-dried tomatoes
- 8.0 oz pesto, prepared
- .25 cup parsley, fresh and chopped up
- 2.0 tbsp olive oil
- 5.0 cups of spaghetti squash, or 1 spaghetti squash

## Instructions:

1. Heat up the oven to exactly 400 degrees Fahrenheit.
2. Take a big knife and split the squash in half.
3. Spread the olive oil evenly over the top of the exposed flesh of the spaghetti squash.
4. Place the squash onto a large baking sheet and bake the squash for 40 minutes.
5. Take it out of the oven to cool to the side until it's cooled down enough to touch it, but is still warm.
6. Use a fork to scrape out spaghetti noodle-like shreds of squash and collect them in a bowl.
7. Dump in the tomatoes, parsley, and pesto and mix it up.
8. Serve it up!

# Enchilada Casserole

How many people it serves: 6
Time to prepare and cook this recipe: 40 minutes
Calorie content: approx. 245

## Ingredients:

- 8.0 corn tortillas
- 1.0 cup of shredded Mexican cheese
- 1.5 cups of enchilada sauce
- 38.0 oz of shredded fully cooked chicken

## Instructions:

1.   Ensure that your oven is at a temperature of exactly 350 degrees Fahrenheit to begin.
2.   Find a glass baking or casserole dish of rectangular shape and coat it thoroughly with cooking spray.
3.   Take half of the cheese and half of the sauce and dump it into a bowl with the chicken, then combine them.
4.   Line the bottom of the glass dish with four of the tortillas.
5.   Dump the chicken mixture over top of the tortillas, then place the remaining tortillas on top.
6.   Pour the rest of the sauce over the tortillas and scatter the remaining cheese atop that.
7.   Take aluminum foil and drape it over the top of the dish, tucking in the corners, and place the dish into the heated oven.
8.   Leave the dish in the oven for about thirty-five minutes until the contents of the dish are heated thoroughly.
9.   Take the dish from the oven carefully and set it aside to cool.
10.  Enjoy!

# Buttered Chicken
# With Potatoes

How many people it serves: 6
Time to prepare and cook this recipe: 45 minutes
Calorie content: approx. 450

## Ingredients:

- 1.0 tsp of olive oil
- .16 oz of cut up potatoes
- 4.0 tbsp butter, warmed until soft
- 6.0 breasts of chicken

## Instructions:

1. Season the potatoes to your preferred taste, as well as the chicken.
2. Ensure that the oven is at the optimal temperature of exactly 300 degrees Fahrenheit.
3. Massage the chicken with the butter all over.
4. Dump the potatoes into a bowl with the oil and shake them around until the potatoes are covered completely.
5. Dump the potatoes onto a baking sheet and top the potatoes with the chicken.
6. Place the baking sheet into the oven for twenty-five minutes, then turn up the temperature to 450 degrees Fahrenheit and continue for fifteen more minutes before removing the baking sheet from the oven.
7. Set the baking sheet on the counter so its contents can cool, then serve.

# Shrimp and Cauliflower
# Mock Grits

How many people it serves: 2
Time to prepare and cook this recipe: 15 minutes
Calorie content: approx. 500

## Ingredients:

- 12.0 oz of cauliflower, frozen
- 1.0 garlic clove, chopped up
- 4.0 tbsp of butter
- 1.0 pound of deveined and peeled shrimp

## Instructions:

1. Season the shrimp to your preferences. Many like Cajun seasoning.
2. Boil one to two inches of water in a pan of your choosing.
3. Allow the cauliflower and garlic to be steamed within the pan until they are at a softened textural state.
4. Dump the cauliflower and garlic into a food processing device with half of the butter and allow them to be stirred until they are thoroughly made into the consistency of rice.
5. Dab the shrimp with a paper towel to get any excess moisture off the surface.
6. Bring the temperature of a pan to a hot temperature and add the rest of the butter so that it will be melted.
7. Dump in the shrimp and allow it to heat until pink in color.
8. Take the pan from the heat and remove the shrimp.
9. Fill two bowls with the cauliflower, garlic, and shrimp. Then enjoy!

# Delightful Turkey Panini

How many people it serves: 4
Time to prepare and cook this recipe: 15 minutes
Calorie content: approx. 370

## Ingredients:

- 4.0 oz of your choice of cheese, sliced into 1.0 oz slices
- 8.0 oz of sliced turkey
- 4.0 or more slices of cooked bacon
- 3.0 tbsp of mayonnaise
- 8.0 pieces of whole-grain bread

## Instructions:

1. Turn on your waffle maker or panini maker.
2. Wait until it reaches the optimal temperature.
3. Assemble your sandwich out of the ingredients provided, including extra ingredients if you so choose, to your preference.
4. Place the sandwich you have concocted into the waffle or panini maker, then press the appliance down onto the sandwich and heat up until it's nice and toasty.
5. Enjoy your sandwiches!

# Hummus and Veggie
# Lunch Wraps

How many people it serves: 2
Time to prepare and cook this recipe: 10 minutes
Calorie content: approx. 260

## Ingredients:

- 1.0 oz of crumbly cheese, such as feta
- 1.0 cup of fresh spinach
- 1.0 sliced bell pepper
- .5 cup of preferred hummus variety
- 2.0 flatbreads or whole-wheat wraps

## Instructions:

1. Smear the hummus across the surface of the wrap.
2. Assemble the wraps with the remaining ingredients, dividing evenly among the two wraps.
3. Roll the wraps up into the sufficient positions, then enjoy!

# Grilled Pepper Tilapia Taco

How many people it serves: 4
Time to prepare and cook this recipe: 30 minutes
Calorie content: approx. 300

## Ingredients:

- 8.0 corn tortillas
- 4.0 tilapia fillets
- 8.0 oz of bell peppers
- 1.0 sliced up onion

## Instructions:

1. Turn on your grill.
2. Coat the grill with cooking spray.
3. Toss all of the vegetables on the grill and sprinkle them with seasonings of your choosing.
4. Take the vegetables off of the grill and chop them up once they are at a reasonable temperature at which you can handle them.
5. Raise the temperature of a skillet to a hot enough level to fry fish.
6. Heat the tilapia for three minutes before flipping and repeat the process.
7. Remove the tilapia from the pan and slide the fillets onto the tortillas.
8. Arrange the vegetables onto the tortillas alongside the tilapia.
9. Serve and enjoy!

# Sweet-and-Spicy Pork

How many people it serves: 4
Time to prepare and cook this recipe: 30 minutes
Calorie content: approx. 175

## Ingredients:

- 1.0 16.0 oz pork tenderloin
- .5 tsp cinnamon, ground
- 2.0 tbsp Worcestershire sauce
- 2.0 tbsp bourbon
- 2.0 tbsp granulated sugar

## Instructions:

1. Warm up the grill to a sufficient temperature.
2. Dump the bottom four ingredients into a bag, seal it, and shake it around until everything is nice and unified.
3. Toss the port into the bag and repeat the shaking process.
4. Toss the pork onto the grill and heat it up for ten minutes, sprinkling the leftover marinade across the top of the pork periodically.
5. Take the pork off the grill and slice it up for everyone to enjoy!

# Tropical Steak

How many people it serves: 4
Time to prepare and cook this recipe: 30 minutes
Calorie content: approx. 380

## Ingredients:

- 18.0 oz cooked rice, brown
- 8.0 oz sliced pineapple, canned or fresh
- 4.0 4.0 oz beef tenderloin fillets
- .25 cups of soy sauce

## Instructions:

1. Take a plastic bag and pour everything inside except for the pineapple and rice.
2. Shake the bag up, so everything inside is combined and covered adequately.
3. Knead the marinade into the beef and flip the bag every few minutes to get it nice and soaked.
4. Spray the grill down with a cooking spray and toss the pineapple onto the grill to char.
5. Take the pineapple off the heat and chop it up nice and little so it will fit atop the steak.
6. Warm the rice and place it on four plates.
7. Grill the steak until it is done to your liking and your preferences.
8. Plate the steak alongside the rice and scatter the pineapple atop the steak for a tropical finish.

# Black Bean and Beef Chili

How many people it serves: 6
Time to prepare and cook this recipe: 30 minutes
Calorie content: approx. 200

## Ingredients:

- 15.0 oz prepared tomato sauce
- 14.0 oz beef broth
- 14.0 oz corn
- 14.0 oz black beans
- 1.0 pound of ground beef mixed with chili powder

## Instructions:

1. Dump the seasoned beef into a Dutch oven. Raise the temperature to a moderately hot level and leave the beef within the oven until it becomes brown and crumbly.
2. Remove the excess moisture and oil from the Dutch oven by delicately draining it.
3. Combine the drained beef with the remaining ingredients and allow it to heat to a boiling temperature.
4. Decrease the temperature to facilitate simmering and sustain it for ten minutes.
5. Remove the lid of the Dutch oven and continue simmering for five additional minutes.
6. Stir the chili.
7. Spoon the chili into six bowls and serve.

# Corn-Bacon Chowder

How many people it serves: 6
Time to prepare and cook this recipe: 15 minutes
Calorie content: approx. 215

## Ingredients:

- .75 cups of sharp cheddar cheese shreds
- 2.0 cups of milk
- 32.0 oz corn
- .5 cup vegetable mix that includes celery and onion
- 2.0 pieces of bacon, cooked and crumbled

## Instructions:

1. Heat the vegetable mix and half of the corn in a pan and stir it until it is nice and warm.
2. Dump half the milk and the remainder of the corn into your favorite blender and blend it until it has a soupy consistency.
3. Pour the corn mixture into the pan with the veggies and add the last of the milk along with the cheese.
4. Warm the mixture over moderate heat while stirring repetitively, making sure not to let the liquid bubble.
5. Wait until the cheese liquefies, then pour the chowder into six bowls and serve hot.

# Microwave Butternut
# Squash Risotto

How many people it serves: 4
Time to prepare and cook this recipe: 25 minutes
Calorie content: approx. 325

## Ingredients:

- 6.0 tbsp grated parmesan cheese
- 12.0 oz butternut squash puree
- 2.5 cups of chicken broth
- 2.0 tsp olive oil
- 1.25 cups of Arborio rice

## Instructions:

1. Toss the rice and oil into a bowl and microwave them for three minutes.
2. Pour in the broth and add water to the rice and continue microwaving for nine more minutes.
3. Stir, then repeat for six additional minutes.
4. Take the bowl out and let the mixture settle for about five more minutes.
5. Microwave the squash in a separate bowl for two minutes.
6. Toss the squash into the rice along with the cheese, and mix them all up.
7. You have risotto!

# Garlic Parmesan Chicken

How many people it serves: 4
Time to prepare and cook this recipe: 35 minutes
Calorie content: approx. 500

## Ingredients:

- 4.0 separated cups of marinara sauce
- 3.0 tbsp of olive oil
- 1.0 cup of grated parmesan cheese
- .66 cup of bread crumbs
- 4.0 breasts of chicken

## Instructions:

1. Ensure that you raise the temperature of your oven to 400 degrees Fahrenheit.
2. Find your preferred baking dish and grease it with cooking spray.
3. Pick a small bowl and put the oil into it.
4. Toss the bread crumbs and the parmesan cheese around in a separate bowl.
5. Dunk the chicken in the oil, then transfer it to the parmesan breadcrumbs and flip it around, so it's covered on its entire surface.
6. Put the coated chicken into the baking dish.
7. Toss the baking dish in the oven and heat for thirty minutes.
8. Take the baking dish out and set it aside to cool before serving.

# Teriyaki and Honey Coated Salmon

How many people it serves: 2
Time to prepare and cook this recipe: 20 minutes
Calorie Content: approx. 300

## Ingredients:

- 2.0 fillets of salmon
- 1.0 minced clove of garlic
- 1.0 piece of ginger, grated
- 2.0 tbsp of soy sauce
- 3.0 tbsp of natural honey

## Instructions:

1. Ensure that your oven is brought to a temperature of exactly 320 degrees Fahrenheit.
2. Warm the honey, ginger, garlic, soy sauce, and a splash of water in your preferred pan at a moderate temperature until it begins to bubble.
3. Once half of the liquid has evaporated, move the pan over to a cool burner.
4. Lay some parchment paper over a baking sheet, then place the salmon atop that.
5. Drizzle half of the glaze over the top of the salmon.
6. Heat the salmon for ten minutes.
7. Remove the baking sheet from the oven.
8. Set the sheet on the counter and dump the rest of the sauce over the salmon.
9. Serve warm, and enjoy!

# Cauliflower Chili

How many people it serves: 4
Time to prepare and cook this recipe: 5 hours including the crockpot
Calorie content: approx. 450

## Ingredients:

- 1.0 head of cauliflower
- 2.0 tomatoes
- 60.0 oz of kidney beans without the salt
- 1.0 pound of ground beef, browned
- Preferred seasonings such as chili powder, paprika, and powdered garlic and onion.

## Instructions:

1. Make sure that the ground beef is heated thoroughly and of a brown color to ensure that it is not raw at the time that you use it for the chili.
2. Sprinkle in any seasonings you would like for the meat at this time.
3. Use your favorite knife and convert all of the vegetables to a chopped state.
4. Toss the chopped cauliflower into your food processor and turn it into a rice-textured state.
5. Pull out your favorite crockpot and dump all of the ingredients into it.
6. Allow the crockpot to warm the chili for four hours at its highest temperature.

# Greek Pot Pie

How many people it serves: 4
Time to prepare and cook this recipe: 40 minutes
Calorie content: approx. 250

## Ingredients:

- 2.0 frozen pie crusts
- 2.0 eggs
- 4.0 oz of crumbly feta cheese
- 6.0 oz of tomatoes that have been sun-dried and suspended in oil
- 7.0 oz of spinach, cooked

## Instructions:

1. Ensure that the oven's temperature is properly raised to exactly 350 degrees Fahrenheit.
2. Take the spinach and the tomatoes and cut them up into a chopped state.
3. Take a paper towel and soak up any extra moisture from the two aforementioned ingredients.
4. Pick out your favorite mixing bowl and toss in the spinach and tomatoes, as well as the eggs and feta cheese.
5. Toss those ingredients together until uniformly shaken together. Ensure that the egg yolk has broken and assimilated itself into the overall concoction of ingredients.
6. Take one pie crust and fill it with the mixture in a pie pan.
7. Take some of the oil from the tomatoes and cover exposed parts of the crust with it, as well as the second crust not yet assembled.
8. Take the second crust and place it over the top of the filled crust, tucking the edges in to ensure that it is sealed correctly.
9. Discard any excess crust that you will not need for the pie covering.
10. Place the entire pie into the oven for thirty minutes to allow for the pie to warm and the crust to perfectly golden in color.
11. Extract the pie from the oven and set it on the counter to lower in temperature.
12. Do not serve until the pie is able to be touched with a bare hand, lest you burn your mouth.

# Stuffed Peppers to the Mex

How many people it serves: 4
Time to prepare and cook this recipe: 40 minutes
Calorie content: approx. 470

## Ingredients:

- 3.0 bell peppers cut in half
- 16.0 oz of cooked rice
- 6.0 slices of preferred cheese
- 15.0 oz rinsed black beans
- 6.0 oz of guacamole

## Instructions:

1. Properly raise the internal temperature of the oven to exactly 400 degrees Fahrenheit.
2. De-seed the inside of the bell peppers.
3. Pull out your baking sheet of preference and place the peppers upon it.
4. Warm the peppers in the oven for twenty minutes exactly.
5. Toss the rice and beans together in a bowl of your choosing.
6. Remove the baking sheet from within the oven and stuff the pepper halves with the rice and bean mixture.
7. Place a single slice of cheese upon each pepper half.
8. Return the baking sheet to the oven for ten minutes.
9. Remove the sheet from the oven and set it on the counter.
10. Put a dollop of guacamole on each pepper and enjoy while they are warm, but not too hot.

# Mushroom Cream Pasta

How many people it serves: 4
Time to prepare and cook this recipe: 25 minutes
Calorie content: approx. 500

## Ingredients:

- 3.0 oz of crumbly blue cheese
- 6.0 oz of spinach
- 14.0 oz of spaghetti noodles
- 8.0 oz of sliced up button mushrooms
- 6.0 pieces of bacon

## Instructions:

1. Place the spaghetti noodles into your pot of preference with an adequate level of water with which you cover the noodles.
2. Allow the water to bubble and soften the pasta to the specification of the box it came from.
3. Heat the bacon pieces in a pan for exactly five minutes.
4. Include the mushrooms and leave them in the pan also for three minutes more.
5. Once the pasta has spent its required span of time within the bubbling water, remove it and allow the water to spill out through a colander.
6. Toss the pasta into the pan along with your other ingredients, adding the cheese, and reduce the temperature within the pan to a cooler setting.
7. Allow the cheese to meld to the pasta, then move the pan to an unheated burner and allow the pasta to sit until you are ready to consume it.

# Quesadilla With Chicken and Alfredo

How many people it serves: 1
Time to prepare and cook this recipe: 10 minutes
Calorie content: approx. 470

## Ingredients:

- 5 cup of pre-cooked chicken
- .33 cup of mozzarella cheese shreds
- .25 cup of Alfredo sauce
- 1.0 tortilla of your choice

## Instructions:

1. Put the tortilla in your preferred pan and toss the rest of the ingredients on top of it.
2. Fold the tortilla over, so the internal ingredients are no longer exposed.
3. Warm on both sides until the cheese begins to soften and pour from the sides of the tortilla.
4. Slide the quesadillas onto your favorite plate and allow them to lower in temperature before indulging!

# Chapter 3

## Snacks and Appetizers

Feeling a little snacky? Need to find that best appetizer to go along with your daily meal? Look no further. Snack on these nutrient-filled, scrumptious snacks to curb your hunger and seize the day!

### Roasted Squash and Zucchini Bowl

How many people it serves: 3
Time to prepare and cook this recipe: 40 minutes
Calorie content: approx. 90

**Ingredients:**

- 2.0 cloves of minced garlic
- 1.0 tbsp olive oil
- .5 chopped red onions
- 2.0 chopped zucchinis
- 2.0 chopped summer squash

**Instructions:**

1. Heat the oven to exactly 425 degrees Fahrenheit.
2. Toss all of the ingredients into a bowl and shake it around to mix it up, or use a spoon. Make sure enough oil has covered the veggies, so they cook properly.
3. Dump the mixture onto a baking sheet, then spread the veggies out evenly.
4. You can add salt and pepper to satiate your taste preferences if you would like.
5. Bake the veggies in the oven for 30 minutes, stirring the veggies around about halfway through.
6. Take the baking sheet out of the oven and let the zucchini and squash cool before serving and eating.

# Crispy Baked Kale Chips

How many people it serves: 1
Time to prepare and cook this recipe: 25 minutes
Calorie content: approx. 185

## Ingredients:

- 5.0 cups, or one bunch, of kale, washed and dried out
- 1.0 tbsp of olive oil
- .5 tsp of sea salt

## Instructions:

1. Make sure to heat up your oven to exactly 350 degrees Fahrenheit.
2. Take the stems out of the leaves of kale and chop up the remaining bits of kale.
3. Toss the kale into a big bowl and shake in the olive oil, making sure to coat the leaves of kale. Then, sprinkle in some salt and shake it all up.
4. Take out a big baking sheet and shake the kale leaves out of the bowl and brush them out into an even layer onto the baking sheet.
5. Put the baking sheet into the heated oven and leave it to bake for fifteen minutes.
6. Take the sheet out and wait until it decreases in temperature from hot to warm, then serve.

# Homemade Healthy
# Pita Crisps

How many people it serves: 4
Time to prepare and cook this recipe: 15 minutes
Calorie content: approx. 235

## Ingredients:

- 1.0 tsp salt, preferably sea salt
- 1.0 tsp powdered garlic
- 2.0 tbsp olive oil
- 3.0 whole pitas, whole wheat

## Instructions:

1. Heat up your oven to exactly 400 degrees Fahrenheit.
2. Slice up your pitas into four equal segments, using either scissors or a sharp knife.
3. Stir up the garlic, salt, and oil in a little bowl.
4. Carefully and evenly brush the oil concoction onto the pita segments.
5. Spread the pita segments evenly onto a baking sheet.
6. Once the oven is fully heated, place the baking sheet into it and let it bake for five minutes on each side.
7. Pull the pita segments out of the oven and let them chill at room temperature until they are cool enough to pick up and munch!

# Honey Oat Energy Balls

How many people it serves: 20
Time to prepare and cook this recipe: 20 minutes
Calorie content: approx. 135

## Ingredients:

- 1.0 tsp vanilla
- .25 cup of natural honey
- .75 cup of peanut butter, creamy in texture
- 2.5 cups of oats

## Instructions:

1. Toss all of the ingredients into your favorite mixing bowl.
2. Mush it all together with your hands until it's nice and uniformly composed.
3. Take chunks of the oat mixture and roll them into smooth balls.
4. Place the energy balls into a container of your choice and enjoy at your leisure.

# One-Ingredient
# Cheese 'Crackers'

How many people it serves: 2
Time to prepare and cook this recipe: 20 minutes
Calorie content: approx. 200

## Ingredients:

- 4.0 slices of very thin, extra sharp cheddar cheese

## Instructions:

1. Ensure that your oven is heated to a temperature of exactly 300 degrees Fahrenheit.
2. Slice the cheese into 16 equal squares to make your cracker shapes.
3. Put the cheese onto a parchment paper-covered baking sheet. Make sure that the cheese is spaced out well, so it doesn't melt into one big glob of cheese.
4. Warm the cheese up in the properly heated oven for fifteen minutes.
5. Take the cheese out of the oven and let them cool down and harden into a cracker-like texture.
6. Snack away!

# Delightful Fruit
# Dipping Sauce

How many people it serves: 6
Time to prepare and cook this recipe: 5 minutes
Calorie content: approx. 130

## Ingredients:

- 1.0 tbsp natural honey
- .33 cup of peanut butter, preferably creamy
- 11.0 oz of Greek Yogurt, vanilla or other preferred flavors

## Instructions:

1. Dump all of the components into your favorite mixing bowl and combine them until they are a smooth consistency.
2. Chop up your favorite fruits, and scoop out the dip. Enjoy!

# Cheesy Spinach Bites

How many people it serves: 20
Time to prepare and cook this recipe: 45 minutes
Calorie content: approx. 50

## Ingredients:

- 1.0 cup of almond flour
- 1.0 tsp of powdered garlic
- 1.0 cup of mozzarella or parmesan cheese
- 3.0 eggs, beaten
- 6.0 cups of spinach without the stems, boiled

## Instructions:

1. Ensure that the oven is at the exact temperature of 370 degrees Fahrenheit.
2. Make sure the cooked spinach is drained adequately before proceeding.
3. Slice up the spinach on a cutting board, so it's nice and fine.
4. Dump the spinach into a bowl with the remaining ingredients and stir it around nicely.
5. Use your hands and scoop out increments of the mixture to mold into balls.
6. Take out your preferred baking sheet and place the spinach bites onto it with even spacing.
7. Heat them in the oven for twenty-five minutes.
8. Remove the baking sheet from the oven and let the temperature of the spinach bites lower until they are safe to pick up.
9. Enjoy!

# Flat Zucchini Bites

How many people it serves: 14
Time to prepare and cook this recipe: 20 minutes
Calorie content: approx. 100

## Ingredients:

- 2.0 tbsp olive oil
- .33 cup of finely chopped onions
- 2.0 beaten eggs
- .66 cup of flour, all-purpose
- 4.0 cups of noodle zucchini

## Instructions:

1. Dry out the zucchini by scattering some salt over it and laying it down on some paper towel to draw out the water from within the vegetable. Then press another paper towel on top of that, and try to use the pressure from your hands to release more moisture and dab it off afterward.
2. Find your favorite mixing bowl and toss in the zucchini with the remaining ingredients, leaving out the olive oil.
3. Combine the ingredients all together, so they are uniform.
4. Take out a large plate of your preference and place a few paper towels on its surface.
5. Take a pan out and raise the temperature of a burner to a moderate level, then place the pan upon it.
6. Pour the olive oil into the pan and allow it to reach a moderate temperature.
7. Form small biscuit-sized amounts of zucchini in your hands.
8. Place the zucchini bites into the oil and allow them to golden in the heat of the oiled pan.
9. Remove the zucchini bites from the oil once they are completed and place them on the prepared plate with the paper towels.
10. Once the bites have reached a safe temperature, you may enjoy!

# 15-Minute Healthy Rolls

How many people it serves: 15
Time to prepare and cook this recipe: 30 minutes
Calorie content: approx. 70

## Ingredients:

- 3.5 cups of flour
- 1.0 egg
- .33 cup of and oil of your choice
- 2.0 tbsp of instant yeast, dissolved in 1.25 cups of water
- .25 cup of granulated sugar

## Instructions:

1. Put the yeast-water into your preferred mixing bowl.
2. Dump in the sugar, oil, egg, and flour and stir them around until they are of a doughy consistency.
3. Knead the dough into your hands and create roll-sized lumps.
4. Grease a cake pan of your choice.
5. Put the uncooked rolls into the cake pan.
6. Ensure that the oven is heated to a temperature of exactly 375 degrees Fahrenheit.
7. While the oven reaches the optimal temperature, let the rolls sit and rise to the necessary height over the course of fifteen minutes.
8. Put the cake pan into the oven and allow the rolls to golden for fifteen minutes.
9. Take the pan out of the oven and serve the rolls at your leisure.

# 5-Minute Coleslaw

How many people it serves: 4
Time to prepare and cook this recipe: 5 minutes
Calorie content: approx. 240

## Ingredients:

- 1.5 tbsp of apple cider vinegar
- 1.5 tbsp of natural honey or your choice of sugars
- .5 cup of your preferred type of mayonnaise
- 14.0 oz of coleslaw mix

## Instructions:

1. Take out two of your favorite mixing bowls. In one, pour in the coleslaw mix and set aside. In the other, dump in the remaining ingredients and stir thoroughly.
2. Add the mayonnaise concoction to the bowl with the coleslaw mix, then toss until the coleslaw mix is covered in the mayonnaise.
3. Spoon the coleslaw into four bowls, and enjoy!

# Crunchy Tortilla Chips

How many people it serves: 6
Time to prepare and cook this recipe: 25 minutes
Calorie content: approx. 200

## Ingredients:

- 20.0 corn tortillas, thin variety
- 4.0 cups of your preferred vegetable oil
- An estimated dash of sea salt to sprinkle atop the finished chips

## Instructions:

1. Warm the oil in a pan of your choice until it reaches no hotter of a temperature than 340 degrees Fahrenheit.
2. Prepare a platter with a few layers of paper towels to soak up the oil from the finished chips.
3. Separate the tortillas into chip shapes.
4. Very rapidly drop the tortilla bits into the heated oil, then flip them as soon as their edges begin to curve upward.
5. Once both sides have warmed and hardened to a crispy state, which should take no more than one minute for each pan-full, take the chips out of the pan before they char.
6. Place the chips onto the paper towel-layered platter.
7. Scatter the sea salt over the platter to adequately season the chips to your preferences. You may leave this step out if you do not like the extra sodium.
8. That's it!

# Italian Garlic Bread

How many people it serves: 10
Time to prepare and cook this recipe: 15 minutes
Calorie content: approx. 180

## Ingredients:

- 3.0 tbsp Italian mix seasoning
- 1.0 tbsp minced garlic
- .5 cup of salted, warmed butter
- 1.0 loaf of French bread, sliced in half long-ways

## Instructions:

1. Raise the temperature of the oven until it is exactly 350 degrees Fahrenheit.
2. Incorporate the garlic and seasoning into the soft, warmed butter in a bowl of your choice.
3. Take out a baking sheet of your preference and lay the bread atop it.
4. Apply the butter mixture to the surface of the bread.
5. Stick the baking sheet into the oven at the topmost rack.
6. Allow the bread to warm at that temperature for three minutes.
7. Separate the bread into equal segments with a knife, then serve.

# Cool-As-A-Cucumber Salad

How many people it serves: 8
Time to prepare and cook this recipe: 45 minutes
Calorie content: approx. 70

## Ingredients:

- .5 cup of sliced red onion
- 1.0 tbsp of dill
- 1.0 tbsp of mayonnaise of your preference
- 2.0 tbsp of olive oil
- 32.0 oz of sliced cucumbers

## Instructions:

1. Take the dill, mayonnaise, and oil and dump them into a bowl, moving them around with a spoon until they are properly distributed evenly throughout.
2. Put the cucumber slices and the onion slices onto a few paper towels, then pat them down with another paper towel to get some of the moisture from their surface.
3. Pick up the vegetables and toss them into the bowl with the mayonnaise mixture, and cover them adequately with the mixture.
4. You can optionally season the salad with spices of your choice or eat as-is.

# Colors of the Rainbow
## Fruit Salad

How many people it serves: 10
Time to prepare and cook this recipe: 20 minutes
Calorie content: approx. 125

## Ingredients:

- 16.0 oz of strawberries
- 3.0 oranges
- 16.0 oz of pineapple
- 4.0 kiwis
- 12.0 oz of blueberries

## Instructions:

1. Wash and chop or slice up all of your various fruits. The only fruits you should not cut are the blueberries.
2. Dump all of the prepared fruit into your favorite serving bowl, and you're all set!

# Artichoke-Spinach Dip

How many people it serves: 8
Time to prepare and cook this recipe: 30 minutes
Calorie content: approx. 240

## Ingredients:

- 6.0 oz thawed frozen spinach
- 14.0 oz of chopped artichoke hearts
- 8.0 oz warmed, soft cream cheese
- .5 cup of sour cream
- .66 cup of shredded parmesan cheese

## Instructions:

1. Ensure that the oven is at a temperature of exactly 350 degrees Fahrenheit.
2. Toss the sour cream, parmesan, and cream cheese into a bowl and combine them.
3. Fold in the artichoke hearts and the spinach.
4. Transfer the mixture into a sprayed baking dish.
5. Place the dish into the oven for twenty minutes.
6. Remove the dish from the oven and let cool to a warm but safe temperature before partaking.
7. If you prefer, you can season with additional amounts of powdered garlic, onion, and black pepper.

# Holiday Cheese Ball

How many people it serves: 16
Time to prepare and cook this recipe: 70 minutes
Calorie content: approx. 215

## Ingredients:

- 1.0 tsp of powdered garlic and onion mix
- 1.0 cup of chopped pecans
- 16.0 oz soft cream cheese
- .33 cup of sour cream
- 8.0 oz of cheddar cheese shreds

## Instructions:

1. Smooth and combine all of the ingredients with the exception of the pecans in your favorite mixing bowl with a hand mixer.
2. Put the bowl into the fridge for one hour to get it hard and ready for forming.
3. Take the cheese mixture into your hands and roll it into a big ball.
4. Toss the cheese ball into a bowl with the pecans and let them scatter over the surface of the ball until it is covered.
5. Serve the cheese ball with a butter knife for easy access and spreading.

# Cheesy Spinach-Filled Mushrooms

How many people it serves: 10
Time to prepare and cook this recipe: 30 minutes
Calorie content: approx. 150

## Ingredients:

- 12.0 oz thawed frozen spinach
- 20.0 de-stemmed button mushrooms
- 8.0 oz of soft cream cheese
- .75 cup of parmesan cheese shreds
- 1.5 tsp of olive oil

## Instructions:

1. Ensure that the oven is at a temperature of exactly 400 degrees Fahrenheit.
2. Lay out the spinach on some paper towels to dry off the excess water.
3. Take a baking sheet and place the mushrooms upon it.
4. Spray the entire sheet with a cooking spray of your choice, including the surface of the mushrooms.
5. Take the cream cheese and spinach and stuff the mushrooms with them.
6. Toss the parmesan with the olive oil in a little bowl of your choosing.
7. Scatter the parmesan over the surface of the filled mushrooms.
8. Put the baking sheet into the oven for twenty minutes until the mushrooms reach an agreeable temperature.
9. Remove the baking sheet from the oven and set aside to lower the mushrooms' temperature to a safe level before serving.

# Chapter 4

## Desserts

Everyone needs a little indulgence, even those on a diet. These desserts are low-calorie, low-sugar, and high in delicious flavor! Stay on course with your fasting journey while enjoying the small, sweet treasures in life we like to call deserts!

## Date-Caramel Coconut Apple 'Cookies'

How many people it serves: 2
Time to prepare and cook this recipe: 6 minutes
Calorie content: approx. 120 calories

### Ingredients:

- 1.5 tsp of coconut oil
- 2.0 tbsp of your preferred chocolate chips
- 2.0 tbsp coconut flakes, unsweetened
- 2.0 tbsp of prepared date-caramel
- 1.0 sizeable apple of your choice, sliced into uniform shapes (Honeycrisp apples are great for this recipe!)

### Instructions:

1. Prepare your date-caramel.
2. Throw the flaked coconut into a little pan and toast it at a moderately low temperature for about five minutes. Take care not to burn the coconut, and rapidly stir the flakes with a spoon or spatula to prevent this burning.
3. Spoon out the seeds from the apple slices and make a little hole in the middle.
4. Drizzle or spread your date-caramel on top of each apple slice.
5. Scatter the coconut flakes over the top of the caramel.
6. Melt your chips and coconut oil in the microwave, stirring occasionally.
7. Drizzle the chocolate and coconut mixture over the apple slices.
8. Let cool, and enjoy your 'cookies'!

# Banana Pudding With
# Peanut Butter Surprise

How many people it serves: 8

Time to prepare and cook this recipe: 20 minutes

Calorie content: approx. 475

## Ingredients:

- 4.0 sliced up bananas
- 6.8 oz vanilla pudding mix, instant
- .33 cup peanut butter, creamy
- 16.0 oz of vanilla-flavored almond milk, unsweetened
- 8.0 oz of Greek yogurt, plain

## Instructions:

1. Put the yogurt, the almond milk, and the peanut butter into a mixing bowl and either mix or hand-blend the ingredients together until it reaches a thick consistency.

2. Slowly mix in the instant pudding mix.

3. In a casserole dish or similar receptacle, one-by-one alternately layer the bananas and the pudding.

4. Cool in the refrigerator for at least an hour and a half so the pudding can chill to perfection! Then, enjoy!

# Easy Almond
# Coconut Cookies

How many people it serves: 18
Time to prepare and cook this recipe: 25 minutes
Calorie content: approximately 115 calories

## Ingredients:

- 75 cups condensed sweetened coconut milk, liquified
- 3.0 tbsp almonds, salted and chopped
- 5 cup chocolate chips, dark mini
- 16 oz coconut flakes, unsweetened

## Instructions:

1. Take care and heat the oven to exactly 325 degrees Fahrenheit.
2. Either grease a big baking sheet or cover it with parchment paper.
3. Throw all of your ingredients together in your favorite mixing bowl and stir it all up!
4. Scoop out your cookie dough with a tablespoon and plop it onto your baking sheet.
5. Delicately flatten each ball of cookie dough, so it's in a cookie shape and has the correct depth.
6. Once the oven is heated correctly, place the baking sheet into the oven and let your cookies bake for about twelve minutes.
7. Take your cookies out of the oven once the coconut flakes have turned a nice golden color, then set them aside to cool.
8. Enjoy!

# Protein-Packed Peanut Butter Cookies

How many people it serves: 12

Time to prepare and cook this recipe: 25 minutes

Calorie content: approx. 80

## Ingredients:

- 2.0 tbsp natural honey
- .25 cup applesauce, unsweet
- .5 cup natural peanut butter
- 2.0 hefty tbsp protein powder, vanilla
- 1.0 cup oats

## Instructions:

1. Heat up the oven to exactly 350 degrees Fahrenheit.

2. Pick up your favorite mixing bowl and toss in the oats and protein powder, whisking them together to get them nice and mixed together.

3. In your second favorite mixing bowl, stir up the applesauce, honey, and peanut butter.

4. Dump the second mixture slowly into your favorite mixing bowl, combining the wet and dry mixtures perfectly. Watch out, because you'll need some elbow grease!

5. Roll up that mixture into nice, round little balls of dough.

6. Space the dough balls onto a parchment paper-covered baking sheet.

7. Make a crisscross on each dough ball to press it into its cookie shape.

8. Put the baking sheet into the heated oven and let the cookies bake for ten to twelve minutes.

9. Take the cookies out of the oven and set them to the side to cool. Then you can enjoy!

# Decadent Chocolate
# Candy Dates

How many people it serves: 10
Time to prepare and cook this recipe: 10 minutes
Calorie content: approx. 150

## Ingredients:

- 1.0 tsp of coconut oil
- .5 cup of dark chocolate chips
- .25 cup of peanuts, crushed up
- 2.0 tbsp natural peanut butter
- 10.0 whole dates

## Instructions:

1. De-pit your dates by slicing a slit into each one and pulling out the pit.
2. Take the peanut butter and stuff it inside each date, filling it until it is nearly .5 teaspoons full of peanut butter.
3. Put the chocolate chips and the coconut oil into a bowl and melt them together in the microwave, mixing every few seconds until it is liquified.
4. Take a toothpick and pierce each date, then coat it entirely until the surface is covered in the melted chocolate mixture.
5. Lay out a sheet of parchment paper and carefully plop each date onto the paper.
6. Scatter the peanuts over the top of the dates.
7. Let the dates chill out on the counter until the peanuts settle, then slide them into the fridge until the chocolate sets up completely.
8. Snack away!

# Edible Bird Nests

How many people it serves: 9
Time to prepare and cook this recipe: 10 minutes
Calorie content: approx. 200

## Ingredients:

- 27.0 candy eggs or jelly beans
- .75 cup of your favorite variety of chocolate chips
- 1.5 cups of shredded coconut, unsweetened

## Instructions:

1. Heat your oven up to exactly 400 degrees Fahrenheit.
2. Sprinkle the coconut onto a prepared baking sheet evenly.
3. Toss the baking sheet into the oven to crisp up the coconut and make it golden. Leave it in for no more than ten minutes.
4. Lay the baking sheet on the counter once you take it from the oven so its temperature can lower to a manageable amount.
5. Heat up the chips by increments of fifteen seconds in the microwave to convert them to a liquified state.
6. Bring the bowl out of the microwave and toss in the coconut to stir them together.
7. Spoon bits of the mixture out onto parchment paper and convert them to a circular shape with your hands, so they resemble a bird's nest.
8. Put three candy eggs or jelly beans atop each edible bird nest to complete the recipe.
9. Let them sit and chill on the counter in order to harden before you indulge.

# Chocolate-Covered Banana Peanut Butter Dessert Sandwiches

How many people it serves: 15
Time to prepare and cook this recipe: 15 minutes
Calorie content: approx. 100

## Ingredients:

- 2.0 tsp coconut oil
- .5 cup of dark chocolate, chips or chunks
- .33 cup of natural peanut butter
- 3.0 sliced bananas without the peel

## Instructions:

1. Take out a baking sheet or platter and cover it with parchment paper.
2. Set the banana slices in a grid fashion on the paper.
3. Scoop some peanut butter atop each banana slice.
4. Top the banana and peanut butter pieces with an additional banana slice.
5. Stick the banana sandwiches into the freezer until they get hard.
6. Liquify your chocolate by warming it in the microwave and stirring incrementally.
7. Take your banana sandwiches out of the freezer and dunk each one into the liquid chocolate.
8. Return your banana sandwiches back to the freezer, now chocolate-coated, and let them get hard once more.
9. Pop them out of the freezer and right into your mouth!

# Lemon-Cinnamon
# Marinated Oranges

How many people it serves: 4
Time to prepare and cook this recipe: 10 minutes
Calorie content: approx. 85

## Ingredients:

- .25 tsp of cinnamon spice
- 1.0 tbsp of granulated sugar
- 2.0 tbsp juiced lemon
- 2.0 tbsp no-pulp orange juice
- 4.0 whole, peeled oranges

## Instructions:

1. Peel off the white bits of the oranges with your fingers to make sure only the clear, orange flesh remains.
2. Slice up all of the oranges and divide them among four different containers for serving purposes.
3. Dump all of the ingredients besides the oranges into a bowl and mix them all together until they're nice and combined.
4. Pour the juice and spice mixture over the four servings of oranges and let them sit and soak up the delicious marinade for a while.
5. Once the oranges have steeped in their decadent bath, you can serve them up and enjoy!

# Frozen Banana Mock Sorbet

How many people it serves: 1
Time to prepare and cook this recipe: 5 minutes
Calorie content: approx. 210

## Ingredients:

- 2.0 whole, sliced, frozen bananas

## Instructions:

1. Throw your frozen bananas into your favorite blender and let them stir around until they have a nice, creamy consistency.
2. Pour the blended banana concoction into your favorite dessert dish and enjoy your sweet treat!
3. Top with whatever you would like, just as you would other favorite frozen treats!

# Banana Brownies

How many people it serves: 18
Time to prepare and cook this recipe: 15 minutes
Calorie content: approx. 140

## Ingredients:

- .5 cup of your favorite chocolate chips
- .5 cup of powdered cocoa
- 1.0 cup of your favorite nut butter, such as peanut or almond
- 6.0 whole bananas, peel off

## Instructions:

1. Ensure that your oven is heated to exactly 350 degrees Fahrenheit.
2. Take out your favorite mixing bowl and toss in your bananas. Mush them down well until they are nice and soft.
3. Drop in the rest of the ingredients listed and stir them adequately until they are blended well.
4. Find a square baking pan and either grease it with cooking spray or butter or line it with parchment paper.
5. Fill the pan with the brownie mixture and smooth it over until it is nice and uniform across the surface.
6. Put the pan in the oven and let the brownie mixture heat up for fifteen minutes.
7. Pull the pan out of the oven and test the brownies with a toothpick or similar object and make sure it comes out clean.
8. Once you are sure that the brownies are cooked adequately, set the pan onto the counter to cool until they are safe to touch.
9. Take a knife and segment the pieces evenly with clean, equal lines to separate the brownies into individual servings.
10. Enjoy!

# Decadent Banana Cookies

How many people it serves: 12

Time to prepare and cook this recipe: 10 minutes

Calorie content: approx. 150

## Ingredients:

- .5 cup of your favorite chocolate chips
- .5 cup of your preferred nut butter, such as almond or peanut
- 2.0 cups of oats
- 3.0 whole bananas, ripe, peeled, and mashed

## Instructions:

1. Ensure that you heat your oven to exactly 350 degrees Fahrenheit.
2. Take out your preferred baking sheet and cover it with parchment paper evenly.
3. Bring out your favorite mixing bowl and add in the mashed bananas and all of your remaining ingredients, then stir them around until they are nice and evenly combined.
4. Take small clumps of batter into your hands and roll the batter into round shapes to be formed into cookies.
5. Place each cookie-shaped batter clump onto the lined baking sheet until the tray is full.
6. Place the entire baking sheet into the adequately heated oven.
7. Let the cookies heat up in the oven for ten minutes.
8. Remove the tray from the oven and set it aside to cool down until the cookies are cool enough to pick up and eat!

# Healthy Rice Cereal Bars

How many people it serves: 12
Time to prepare and cook this recipe: 5 minutes
Calorie content: approx. 100

## Ingredients:

- .5 cup of pure maple syrup
- .5 cup of your favorite nut butter, such as peanut or almond
- 2.0 cups of crispy rice cereal

## Instructions:

1. Use butter or parchment paper to cover the inside of a square baking pan completely.
2. Pick out your favorite mixing bowl and dump in the cereal.
3. On your stovetop, take a saucepan and toss in the nut butter and the syrup.
4. Stir the two ingredients together well while you heat the mixture at a moderately low temperature until they melt together well.
5. Add the syrup and nut butter mixture to the mixing bowl with the cereal, and stir them up well until they are combined completely.
6. Take your hands and scoop out the sticky rice cereal mixture, and transfer the mixture to the baking pan until the pan is full.
7. Either eat immediately or put the pan into the fridge to harden up a bit.

# Delicious Apple Oat Cookies

How many people it serves: 12
Time to prepare and cook this recipe: 15 minutes
Calorie content: approx. 150

## Ingredients:

- 1.0 tsp cinnamon or similar spice
- .25 cup of your favorite sweetener
- .5 cup of applesauce, unsweetened
- .5 cup of pureed pumpkin
- 2.0 cups of rolled oats

## Instructions:

- Make sure that you heat your oven up to exactly 350 degrees Fahrenheit.
- Grab your favorite mixing bowl and toss in the applesauce, sweetener, oats, and pumpkin.
- Combine them adequately until they are evenly stirred through.
- Pick up the batter in your hands and roll each handful of batter into the shape of a cookie.
- Place each cookie-shaped handful of batter onto a baking sheet that has been greased.
- Shake the cinnamon over the top of the tray in order to cover the cookies.
- Put the prepared baking sheet into the adequately heated oven and leave them for 10 minutes until they are heated thoroughly.
- Take the tray out of the oven and set it aside to cool down.
- Serve up the cookies and enjoy!

# Healthy Chocolate
# Mug Cake

- How many people it serves: 1
- Time to prepare and cook this recipe: 1 minute
- Calorie content: approx. 100

## Ingredients:

- .25 cup of almond milk
- 2.0 tbsp of your favorite sweetener
- 2.0 tbsp of cocoa powder
- 1.0 egg
- 1.0 whole banana, ripe and peeled

## Instructions:

1. Toss every ingredient into your favorite food processor and blend until the batter is nice and smooth.
2. Grease the inside of your favorite coffee mug.
3. Fill the mug with the cake batter.
4. Microwave the cake batter-filled mug for one minute.
5. Take the mug out of the microwave carefully, let it cool, then enjoy!

# Coconut Balls

How many people it serves: 40
Time to prepare and cook this recipe: 10 minutes
Calorie content: approx. 70

## Ingredients:

- .25 cup of coconut milk
- .75 cup of pure maple syrup
- 24.0 oz of shredded unsweetened coconut
- 1.0 cup of almond flour

## Instructions:

1. Toss the ingredients into your favorite mixing bowl and stir it all up until the dough is evenly combined.
2. If it crumbles a bit, pour in some more coconut milk until the dough is a bit sticky.
3. Roll the mixture into little balls and sprinkle with any remaining coconut shreds.
4. Pop the coconut balls into the fridge until they get nice and hard.
5. Pop them into your mouth!

# Chocolate Peanut Butter
# Frozen Muffin Cups

How many people it serves: 12
Time to prepare and cook this recipe: 45 minutes
Calorie content: approx. 200

## Ingredients:

- 3.0 tbsp coconut oil, melted
- .25 cup of natural honey or pure maple syrup
- .5 cup of peanut butter, creamy
- 1.0 cup of your favorite chocolate chips

## Instructions:

1. Take out a muffin tin and silicone or paper muffin cups.
2. Arrange the cups into the muffin tin.
3. Take the chips and one-third of the oil and combine them into a small bowl of your choosing, liquifying them together in the microwave for one and a half minutes.
4. Fill out the bottom of each of the approximately twelve muffin cups with the chocolate concoction.
5. Put the muffin tins with the chocolate into your freezer for a few minutes to allow the chocolate to harden sufficiently.
6. While this is occurring, put the rest of the coconut oil in another bowl of your choosing, along with the remaining ingredients.
7. Allow these to liquify in the microwave similarly to the chocolate, but for shorter intervals of time with stirring in between.
8. Take out the frozen muffin tin and add the peanut butter mixture to the muffin cups.
9. Put the muffin tin back into your freezer for five more minutes.
10. Remove the muffin tin once more.
11. If there is any chocolate remaining in your first bowl, you may drizzle it over the hardened muffin cups.
12. Return the muffin tin to the freezer until the filled cups harden completely and uniformly.
13. Take the muffin tin out for the last time and pop out all of the muffin cups, filled with the decadent treat.
14. Arrange the treats for all to enjoy! You may want to allow them to come to room temperature before biting into them, however, so they are not too hard for your teeth.

# Coconut-Chocolate Treats

How many people it serves: 16
Time to prepare and cook this recipe: 30 minutes
Calorie content: approx. 200

## Ingredients:

- 2.5 cups of coconut cream
- 3.0 tbsp of pure maple syrup
- .5 cup of chocolate chips of your choice
- 2.0 tbsp of coconut oil
- 2.5 cups of flaked coconut, unsweet

## Instructions:

1. Take some wax paper and lay it inside a square cake pan.
2. Blend the coconut, oil, all but .25 cup of the cream, and the syrup in your favorite blender until the concoction is sticky and moist.
3. Smooth the coconut concoction into the cake pan.
4. Microwave the chips and remaining cream for one minute, incrementally, to liquify them together. Add more time if one minute does not sufficiently achieve this.
5. Put the chocolate mixture atop the coconut concoction, making sure it is uniform across the surface.
6. Place the cake pan into your freezer until it hardens, then segment the treat into manageable parts for serving.

# Date Mock Brownies

How many people it serves: 8
Time to prepare and cook this recipe: 10 minutes
Calorie content: approx. 140

## Ingredients:

- 1.0 tsp of vanilla
- 1.0 tbsp of natural honey
- 3.0 tbsp of powdered cocoa
- 10.0 pitted, chopped up dates
- 1.0 cup of ground up walnuts

## Instructions:

1. Take plastic wrap and cover up a loaf pan with it.
2. Toss all of the ingredients into your food processor and let it process them until they are nice and uniformly combined, dropping in a bit of water if needed for texture purposes.
3. Put the mixture into the loaf pan and press it down with your hands until it forms an adequate load shape within the pan.
4. Cut the loaf into uniform brownie shapes and take them out when you would like to consume them.

CPSIA information can be obtained
at www.ICGtesting.com
Printed in the USA
LVHW060206121020
668549LV00025B/482